Philippians
unrestrained Joy!

Linda Osborne

CONTENTS

PREFACE

❧

The letter to the Philippians is one of the four letters written by the apostle Paul known as the Prison Epistles. It was written around A.D. 61, during his first imprisonment in Rome. When it is considered that he wrote this letter from prison, the contents take on special significance. It is also known as the Epistle of Joy, because the theme of joy is woven throughout the entire letter. In essence, it is a thank you note, written in response to the monetary gift received by Paul from the Philippians through the ministry of Epaphroditus.

Paul founded the church in Philippi in A.D. 51 on his second missionary journey, ten to eleven years before he wrote this letter. Acts 16 reveals the circumstances of Paul's arrival in Philippi. It seems that Paul was revisiting the churches in which he and Barnabas had first proclaimed the Gospel, strengthening them as he went. After passing through Syria and Cilicia, Phrygia and Galatia, his desire was to go to Asia, but he was forbidden by the Holy Spirit to speak the Word there. Passing on to Mysia, and seeking from there to enter Bythinia with the Gospel, once again the Holy Spirit intervened and forbid them to enter. From there, they (Paul, Silas, and Timothy) went on to Troas. It was there that they finally received positive guidance from the Lord as to where they were to go. In a vision, Paul saw a man of Macedonia appealing to him to, "Come over to Macedonia and help us." From this point on, as they went over from Troas to Macedonia, Luke seems to have joined the party.

Sailing from Troas, they went straight to Samothrace, and from there, the following day, to Neapolis and then on to Philippi, a leading city of Macedonia. It is thought that Luke was a native of

Philippi, a town which was originally named after King Philip of Macedonia but was eventually captured by Rome (168 B.C.) and even still later (42 B.C.), made a Roman colony, giving the Philippians special privileges as Roman citizens. It was here that Paul made his first European converts: Lydia (from the city of Thyatira, a seller of purple fabrics, and a worshiper of God) and her household, as well as the Philippian jailer and all his household. You may wish to read the remarkable account of the beginning of the Philippian church in Acts 16. It's a wonderful story and a testimony to the joy of the Lord, which then and always filled Paul.

As you read this joyous letter, keep in mind the key and most significant verse, describing the true heart and motivation of Paul: *"For to me, to live is Christ, and to die is gain"* (Philippians 1:21). Let's pray, as we study Paul's words, that we would gain this same heart attitude and make it our own, to the glory of God!

PHILIPPIANS 1

Day 1
Daily Facts
Read Philippians 1:1-11

1. Who is this letter from, according to verse 1?

As you look over the letter, you will see very quickly that it is written in the first person: from Paul (verse 3: "I thank my God …", verse 6: "For I am confident …"). Timothy was with Paul when he founded the church in Philippi and must have been present as Paul wrote this letter from Rome, maybe even physically writing it as Paul dictated to him.

    a. What does Paul call himself and Timothy?

    b. If Paul and Timothy were Christ's bondservants, what was Christ to them? What does that imply to you? Would you be able to identify yourself as a bondservant of Christ Jesus?

The Greek word for *servant* in this verse is doulos, which means slave. It indicates one who is subject to the will of his master, and completely at his disposal.

The idea of *bondservant* comes from the practice of a slave who has been *set free* remaining at the disposal of his master. It may have been this idea that Paul had in mind as he used this term to describe himself and Timothy—free, yet wholly devoted to the Master.

2. Who is the letter addressed to? (v. 1)

We might think of the word *saints* as referring to those who are sinless. But the Greek word hagioi actually means those who are set apart and includes all who are saved through Jesus Christ. The words *set apart* not only describe who we are in Christ, but they describe what we are to be.

   a.   What does Psalm 4:3 say about being *set apart*?

   b.   Do you recognize yourself as one who is set apart in Christ? Share your thoughts on what this means to you.

3. What blessing does Paul immediately speak to the Philippians? v. 2

   a.   How does he say he thinks of them:

   In verse 3?

   In verse 4?

   b.   Why does he pray this way for them? v. 5

    c. Why does he feel this way about them? v. 7

Two key words pop out in these verses: Paul thanks God in *all* his remembrance of them. He always offers prayer with *joy* in his every prayer for them *all*.

The words *joy* or *rejoice* will appear 16 times in this letter and give us a major theme. The word *all* will appear many times throughout this first chapter of Philippians; Paul bringing the concept of unity (another key theme of this letter) and possibly setting the stage for his word of exhortation to Euodia and Syntyche as seen in chapter 4.

    d. Verse 8 describes more fully how he feels for them. What does he say?

    e. Verse 9 describes the specific way in which he prays for them. What does he pray?

    f. What will be the result for them in answer to this prayer? vv. 10-11

J. B. Phillips translates verse 10 in this way: "I want you to be able always to recognize the highest and the best, and to live sincere and blameless lives until the day of Christ." Life Application Bible notes: "They should have the ability to differentiate between right and wrong, good and bad, healthy and dangerous, vital and trivial; but they should also have the discernment to decide between acceptable and right, good and best, and important and urgent— in other words, to know what really matters."

4. You may have learned to differentiate between good and bad and between healthy and dangerous, but have you learned to discern between vital and trivial? Between good and best? Between important and urgent? Share how being *set apart for God* will make a difference in your understanding of what really matters.

5. In the middle of Paul's expression of love for the Philippians he makes a statement of his confidence in the work of God in their lives. Of what is he confident? v. 6

    a. Do you realize the magnificence of the promise wrapped up in this verse? Think it through for a moment and write your thoughts on what it means to you personally: *"For I am confident of this very thing, that He who began a good work in me will perfect it until the day of Christ Jesus."*

Stone of Remembrance:

"For to me, to live is Christ, and to die is gain." Philippians 1:21

Day 2
Daily Facts
Read Philippians 1:12-26

1. What wonderful statement was Paul able to make in verse 12?

   a. What exactly were his circumstances?

   b. Verse 13 gives us a more definite cause of Paul's imprisonment. In what way does he define his imprisonment?

Paul, who had been in prison for about two years by now, is not in prison for a crime but for his Christianity. Although Paul is in chains, his message of Christ's love is not!

2. Verses 13 and 14 give us two reasons for the progress that has been made. What are they?

While in prison, it was customary for the prisoner to be chained at the wrist to a soldier, who would be replaced every four hours. Not only would Paul have the opportunity to speak personally to these soldiers, but they would hear and witness all that went on between him and those who would visit him.

a. There were two motivations, according to Paul, of those who were now proclaiming the Gospel. What were they? vv. 15-17

   Positive motive:

   Negative motive:

b. What was Paul's response to his understanding of both motivations? v. 18

c. What does this response reveal to you about Paul's own motives and personal ambition?

3. Of what was Paul sure? v. 19

a. What was Paul's one ambition? v. 20

J.B. Phillips translates this verse this way: "... but now as always I should honor Christ with the utmost boldness by the way I live ..." Oswald Chamber's devotion, *My Utmost for His Highest,* is based on this verse and paraphrases Paul's words in this way: "My determination is to be my utmost for His Highest," and interprets them in this way: "Shut out every other consideration and keep yourself before God for this one thing only—My Utmost for His Highest. I am determined to be absolutely and entirely for Him and for Him alone."

b. This was Paul's aim and goal in life. Is it yours? Do you want it to be? It is a matter of the will. Are you *willing* to be your utmost for His Highest? Share your thoughts.

Paul's goal was that *Christ be exalted*—in whatever manner that was necessary—whether by life or whether by death.

4. Why, according to verse 21, was Paul able to make this strong statement?

Keep in mind that verse 21 is the key verse of this letter to the Philippians.

  a. What do you think Paul meant when he said:

  ✝ *To me to live is Christ?* (See verse 22.)

  ✝ *To me to die is gain?* (See verse 23.)

  b. To what conclusion did Paul come in this debate between the possibility of living and dying? vv. 24-26

  c. How does the fact that it made no difference to Paul whether he lived or died affect the way he was able to minister the gospel?

  d. There might be many things that we could say matter most to us: money, success, happiness, material possessions, prestige—but for Paul it was *Christ*. What is it for you? Be honest with yourself. You don't have to share this with your group—but share it with your God and if the answer isn't *Christ*, then ask God to begin a work in your heart to bring you into this holy perspective.

H.A. Ironside says of this verse, "Paul wrote of the life in which Christ so dominates and controls the believer that his one object is to live to His glory." He goes on to add, "This is life in its truest sense, and probably no one ever entered into it so fully as the apostle Paul."

Review this week's memory verse.

Day 3
Daily Facts
Read Philippians 1:27-30

1. Paul begins Philippians 1:27 with the words, "Only conduct yourselves in a manner worthy of the gospel of Christ ..." Why is the Christian's conduct so important? See also Ephesians 4:1

   a. From what we have studied so far, is Paul asking them to do anything that he isn't willing to do? What is Paul able to say in 1 Corinthians 11:1? Would you be able to make this statement to your friends, family, co-workers?

2. What is it that Paul desires to hear of them or see in them in the future? v. 27b

The key thought here is *unity.*

3. Paul spoke similarly to the Ephesians with regard to their unity. What doctrinal truths does he reveal to them in Ephesians 4:4-6?

a. What should our understanding of this result in? Ephesians 4:3

b. Why is Christian unity important according to Paul's final thought in Philippians 1:27?

c. Has it been important to you to maintain unity with your Christian brothers and sisters? Is this an area you need to work on?

As Paul encouraged the Philippians to unity, he also exhorted them to be *courageous* in the face of opposition. This is the first sign that the Philippians were opposed in their faith.

4. According to verse 28, how were they to face this opposition?

a. What would this courageous spirit be a sign of:

To their opponents?

To themselves?

b. Is it possible for you to apply this Scripture to your own situation?

Paul makes a statement in verse 29 that is profound. It goes along with the heart of his letter so far. He says that there are two things granted to the Christian for Christ's sake:

1) To believe in Him ...

The Amplified Bible translates this verse: "For you have been granted [the privilege] for Christ's sake not only *to believe in (adhere to, rely on, and trust in) Him*, but also to suffer in His behalf."

5. Consider this particular translation for a moment, and share your thoughts: Have you realized what a *privilege* it is to believe in Christ? ("For to you it has been granted ...")

   a. Could your belief in Christ be defined by the words that you *adhere to Him, rely on Him,* and *trust in Him*?

2) To suffer for His sake ...

"For you have been granted [the privilege] for Christ's sake not only to believe in (adhere to, rely on, and trust in) Him, *but also to suffer in His behalf.*"

Verse 30 reveals that Paul sees the Philippians sharing in the sufferings of Christ *with him*—experiencing some of the same conflict in which he is engaged. The principle is laid out that Christians will suffer. In 2 Timothy 3:12, Paul actually promises the believer: *"And indeed, all who desire to live godly in Christ Jesus will be persecuted."*

6. Look at the following Scriptures, which speak of our portion in the sufferings of Christ, and share your thoughts on why it is a privilege for the Christian *to suffer in His behalf:*

   ✝ Romans 8:16-17

✠ 2 Corinthians 1:5; 4:10

✠ 1 Peter 4:1, 12-13

7. We've already recognized that Paul's personal motivation in life is *Christ*. How does Paul further reveal this same goal, which fully included sharing in the sufferings of Christ, in Philippians 3:10?

   a. Already in this letter, Paul has given us a high and holy example to follow. Is there a verse in this chapter that best expresses your own personal desire and hope for your walk with Christ? Share it here.

Review this week's memory verse.

Day 4
Overview of Philippians 1

Today we will be looking at the passage we have studied this week as a whole. The goal is to find the main lessons the Lord has for us from this chapter. Don't worry about being clever or profound—just do your best!

Find the Facts ...

1. See if you can state the *content* of this week's passage in a couple of sentences. (Who is speaking, what is taking place, what is the main subject?)

Look for the Heart ...

2. What do you think is the main *lesson* of this chapter? (What spiritual truths are taught here? Look for a command, a word of exhortation, a promise, etc.)

Hear Him Speak ...

3. Look for a *personal application* from the content of this chapter. It should come from the lesson you got from the chapter (question 2). How will you apply the lesson to yourself?

4. Was there a particular verse that ministered to you this week? What was it and how did it minister to you?

5. Write out your stone of remembrance *from memory*!

PHILIPPIANS 2

✤

Day 1
Daily Facts
Read Philippians 2:1-4

Verse 1 of chapter 2 is a continuation of the thought process Paul began in 1:27-30, concerning unity.

1. Paul sets the stage of his appeal to the Philippians' need for humility in order to maintain unity with four "if" statements:

✝ if there is _____

✝ if there is _____

✝ if there is _____

✝ if there is _____

What Paul speaks about here is what the Philippians actually have as believers in Christ, and if you are a Christian you, too, have each of these things. One commentator called them "4 Realities."

2. Since these Christian graces were theirs (and are yours), what should be the four-fold result, which would bring completeness of joy to Paul? v. 2

a. Does being of the same mind with other Christians mean that you will always think exactly the same way and be in constant agreement on every subject? What do you think it means?

A good way to sum up Paul's thought here is *harmony*: Christian harmony in the work of Christ. Paul goes on to show how this harmony can be maintained in verses 3-4, and it is here that we begin to be taught by Paul on the subject of humility.

3. The dictionary definition of humility (a noun) is "the quality or state of being humble." Look up the word humble (an adjective) in your dictionary and see what this word actually means.

One of the key words in defining humility, or the state of being humble, is the word lowly. You might say it is *lowliness of mind*.

✤ How do Paul's words in verses 3-4 actually define the state of being lowly of mind?

✤ Is this an easy thing to do in the world in which we live? Why?

4. The teachings of Christ are in direct opposition to the teachings of the world. Look at Matthew 5:2-10 and share what Jesus taught us:

Blessed are_____

Why?_____

Blessed are_____

Why?_____

Blessed are_____

Why?_____

Blessed are_____

Why?_____

Blessed are_____

Why?_____

Blessed are_____

Why?_____

Blessed are_____

Why?_____

Blessed are_____

Why?_____

It is virtually impossible in our natural selves to be what Jesus teaches here. The only way we can accomplish this is by the Holy Spirit's empowering in our lives. Oswald Chambers says, *"I must know Jesus Christ as Savior before His teaching has any meaning for me other than that of an ideal which leads to despair. But when I am born again of the Spirit of God, I know that Jesus Christ did not come to teach only: He came to make me what He teaches I should be."*

    a.   What important principle of Christian living do you see in these profound words? See James 4:10

b. How does Philippians 2:13 help you understand how you are able to fulfill the teachings of Paul (which are in the spirit of the teachings of Jesus) given in these verses?

Stone of Remembrance:

"... For it is God who is at work in you, both to will and to work for His good pleasure." Philippians 2:13

Day 2
Daily Facts
Read Philippians 2:5-11; 19-30

Example of Humility: Jesus Christ—verses 5-11

1. Considering what Paul has said in verses 3-4, he now gives us the perfect example of the One who has lived this principle out. Exactly what does he say in verse 5?

   a. Again, considering what we have studied so far, of what kind of mind or attitude is Paul speaking?

   b. Look carefully at verses 6-8 and define how it is that Jesus Christ is our supreme example of humility. What does it mean that:

   ✚ *He existed in the form of God?*

   ✚ *He did not regard equality with God a thing to be grasped?*

✞ *He emptied Himself, taking the form of a bond-servant ... in the likeness of man?*

✞ *What was the supreme humility of Jesus?*

The thing we need to be careful to recognize is that, although Jesus took the form of man, He never stopped being God. He emptied Himself of the privileges or prerogatives of Deity, in other words, He gave up His rights as God, but He never ceased to be God. He was fully God and fully man. That is the miracle of the incarnation.

2. How does Romans 15:3a beautifully illustrate the humility of Jesus?

3. Verse 9 is the fulfillment or outcome of this life surrendered to the complete will of the Father. It begins with the word, "therefore." Therefore, because Jesus emptied Himself of his Divine rights and because He humbled Himself to the point of death, even death on a cross—*what did God do?* vv. 9-11

    a. Here is a principle that we touched on yesterday. Matthew 23:12 might say it best in the context of what we are learning in this chapter. What does it tell us?

    b. Look back one verse to Matthew 23:11. How does it, along with Mark 10:45, perfectly describe our supreme model of humility—Jesus Christ?

   c. How will the example of the humility of *Jesus* will affect the outworking of Philippians 2: 3-4 in your life?

Example of Humility: Timothy—verses 19-24

Paul, speaking of his desire to send Timothy to Philippi to help and encourage the believers in their faith, commends him to them and gives us an example of humility.

4. Paul calls Timothy a kindred spirit here in verse 20 and says that he, like Paul, would be genuinely concerned for their welfare. How did Paul describe his own humble service in regard to the Philippians in verse 17?

   a. What did most of those around Paul concern themselves with? v. 21

   b. What did Timothy (like Paul) concern himself with? v. 21

   c. From these verses, see if you can define why Timothy is an example to us of humility (remember again verses 3-4).

Example of humility: Epaphroditus—verses 25-30

Even as Paul writes these words, Epaphroditus stands among the Philippians, as he is the one who has delivered the letter they are reading. Epaphroditus gives us another example of humility.

5. List the words Paul uses to describe Epaphroditus in verse 25.

a. What sense does this already give you as to Paul's regard for him?

b. What was Epaphroditus' concern for the Philippians? v. 26

c. From verses 27 and 30, describe his illness.

d. From these verses, see if you can define why Epaphroditus is an example to us of humility (remembering again verses 3-4).

6. What does Paul exhort them to do in regard to Epaphroditus in verse 29, and how are they to regard men like him?

a. Is there an Epaphroditus in your life? Are you rejoicing in this person? Are you holding him or her in high regard? How have you encouraged your Epaphroditus recently?

Review this week's memory verse.

Day 3
Daily Facts
Read Philippians 2:12-18

In verse 12, we take a turn from theory to practice. The exhortation has been given (verses 3-4), the supreme example has been shared (verses 5-8), now we must work it out!

1. What immediate exhortation does Paul give in verse 12?

    a. Does Paul say to work *for* their salvation here? What does he say?

    b. How does Ephesians 2:8-9 clearly reveal that we are saved by faith not by works?

The Amplified Bible amplifies the words *work out* with the following: cultivate, carry out to the goal, and fully complete. And of *fear and trembling*, it says: with reverence and awe and trembling (self-distrust, with serious caution, tenderness of conscience, watchfulness against temptation, timidly shrinking from whatever might offend God and discredit the name of Christ).

2. Paul says, "For it is *God* who is at work within you ..." Considering the exhortation to humility and our example of humility, why would it be necessary to work out our salvation with fear and trembling?

    a. What is God working in us according to verse 13?

J.B. Phillips translates verse 13 this way: "For it is God who is at work within you, giving you the will and the power to achieve His purpose."

    b. What help does this marvelous verse give you in regard to the working out of your own salvation?

3. What command does Paul give them that is a key to humility in personal relationships? v. 14

    a. How are you doing in the area of complaining and arguing? Is this an area in which you need work? Do you see how it is an outworking of humility? (Notice how this verse works with Paul's teaching in verses 3-4.)

    b. What will they prove by behaving this way? v. 15

    c. Paul describes the generation in which they live as warped and diseased (Phillips). How would you describe the generation in which you live?

Paul says that in the midst of this wicked generation they appear as lights.

4. How does Matthew 5:14 describe you, the Christian, as a light?

    a. Why are you (Christian) the light of the world? See John 8:12.

    b. What should we do with our light according to:

    Matthew 5:15?

    Matthew 5:16?

c. Do you see your life as having this effect? Do you think others see you as blameless, harmless, and faultless, in the midst of this wicked and perverse generation? If not, what might you need to do to fulfill the commands set out by Jesus in Matthew and by Paul in Philippians?

5. What are they to hold fast, according to verse 16? To what does this refer?

There are two ways in which this verse can be understood—first, that they should hold *out* the word of life by spreading the gospel to the dark world around them; second, that they should hold *onto* the word of life as their personal source of truth and light.

a. Are you holding out the word of life to others, so that they might have life?

J.B. Phillips translates verse 16, "For you hold in your hands the very word of life."

b. Do you see the Word of God as the very word of life for *your* life?

c. How would this command (v. 16a) help them to fulfill Paul's words in verses 14-15, as well as Jesus' command in Matthew 5:15?

Paul says that if they do these things, it would give him something to be proud of in the day of Christ, "... for I shall know then that I did not spend my energy in vain." We can add to Paul's joy in that day by taking these principles to heart, living lives in which humility and unity prevail.

Review this week's memory verse.

Day 4
Overview of Philippians 2

Today we will be looking at the passage we have studied this week as a whole. The goal is to find the main lessons the Lord has for us from this chapter. Don't worry about being clever or profound—just do your best!

Find the Facts ...

1. See if you can state the *content* of this week's passage in a couple of sentences. (Who is speaking, what is taking place, what is the main subject?)

Look for the Heart ...

2. What do you think is the main *lesson* of this chapter? (What spiritual truths are taught here? Look for a command, a word of exhortation, a promise, etc.)

Hear Him Speak ...

3. Look for a *personal application* from the content of this chapter. It should come from the lesson you got from the chapter (question 2). How will you apply the lesson to yourself?

4. Was there a particular verse that ministered to you this week? What was it and how did it minister to you?

5. Write out your stone of remembrance *from memory*!

PHILIPPIANS 3

✦

Day 1
Daily Facts
Read Philippians 3:1-11

This entire third chapter of Philippians is pointed heavenward. All of Paul's thoughts and desires are toward and to be fulfilled in heavenly places! To the Colossians, he says it this way, "Set your mind on the things above, not on the things that are on earth. For you have died and your life is hidden with Christ in God" (Colossians 3:2-3). Is this your perspective? We would do well to ask the Holy Spirit to enlighten us to our own spiritual condition as we study this great chapter of Scripture. And "if in anything you have a different attitude, God will reveal that also to you" (Philippians 3:15).

1. What exhortation did Paul not mind repeating once again to his friends, the Philippians?

   a. Even as it was no trouble for him, what would this reminder be for them?

   b. Take a moment and consider why rejoicing in the Lord is a safeguard for the believer.

2. Right here, in verse 2, it seems that Paul's mind is exercised on behalf of the Philippians, as he speaks out three times the word "Beware"! Of what are they to beware?

These dogs that Paul speaks of are most likely the Judaizers, who followed Paul from church to church to undermine his teaching of the grace of Christ. They felt it was their mission to go to those who were being saved by grace and to add the law—most particularly the law of circumcision.

    a. How does Ephesians 2:8-9 clarify how we obtain salvation?

Circumcision was an outward and physical act performed in obedience to God by the sons of Israel. It was a mark of their faith in God. It wasn't their faith, it was a mark of their faith.

3. What does Paul call himself and the Philippians—those who are true believers in Christ? v. 3a

    a. What are the actions and attitudes of true believers in Christ? v. 3

      1.
      2.
      3.

    b. How does Romans 2:29 define what Paul is saying here?

    c. What does Galatians 6:15 say on this subject?

d. Do you understand Paul's point? Share what you understand.

Paul's final emphasis in verse 3 is that true believers put no confidence in the flesh. The Judaizers obviously were putting confidence in what they did. Paul says it's not about us, it's about Jesus Christ!

4. If anyone had a mind to put confidence in the flesh, Paul could have! Make a list of the seven things in which Paul could have had confidence, if he had chosen to put confidence in himself. vv. 4-6

a. Did he put any confidence in these things? How did he perceive them? v. 7

In fact, Paul says, "More than that, I count all things to be loss, in view of the surpassing value of knowing Christ Jesus my Lord …"

b. What was Paul's one desire, according to verse 8?

This concept is profound. Think for a moment about what is most important to you. What is your goal? You have one. What is your value system? Is it your one priority that you might gain Christ?

Paul seemed to recognize that he had a choice. He could have his own righteousness based on the law (which, by the way, he could never fulfill), or he could have the righteousness of Christ that comes from God on the basis of faith.

5. See of you can share what Paul is saying in verse 9 in your own words. What does this mean to you?

6. What, again, from verses 10-11, is Paul's one great aim?

    a. Is this your aim? Consider carefully verses 8 and 10 and share where you stand in relation to the high standard Paul sets here.

Stone of Remembrance:

"I press on toward the goal for the prize of the upward call of God in Christ Jesus." Philippians 3:14

Day 2
Daily Facts
Read Philippians 3:12-16

Paul ends his thoughts in verse 11 with the spoken desire of attaining to the resurrection from the dead. It isn't that Paul is unsure of this future blessing but that it is his aim and desire.

1. Had Paul "arrived" yet, as far as his goal as stated in verses 10-11 was concerned? How did he say this? v. 12a

    a.   What was his attitude toward this? v. 12b

Paul wanted to lay hold of that for which he was laid hold of. He saw that there was purpose in Christ's choice of him. This would be good for us to realize as well.

    b.   Had he laid hold of it yet? v. 13a

Paul's perspective was a good one. He wasn't satisfied with what he had gained in his relationship with Christ. He wanted more! Do you want more? Warren Wiersbe says, "A sanctified dissatisfaction is the first essential to progress in the Christian race."

2. As Paul desired to obtain that which he found to be most valuable in life, he narrowed it down one thing. "But this one thing I do …" What one thing (with three parts!) did Paul do? vv. 13-14

We must make sure to notice that Paul is using an analogy of running a race in these verses. He is pressing on for the prize—reaching forward to what lies ahead and not looking back.

    a.   How would it hinder a runner in his race if he kept looking behind him?

    b.   Can you think of how it could hinder a Christian in his race if he continually set his mind on things from the past?

    c. What personal thoughts might Paul have had in mind when he wrote the words, "forgetting what lies behind"?

    d. What might you need to forget that lies behind?

One of the enemy's greatest tools against the believer is the past. We must not allow him to bring it before us as if it is something we need to fix or continue in guilt over.

A wise man of God once said, "It is a sin to bring out from under the blood of Christ that for which He died." Once forgiven, we are truly forgiven. Let's press on!

3. There is a wonderful promise for us in verse 15. What does Paul say *we* are to do? (v. 15a)

    a. See if you can sum up what attitude that would be.

    b. What does he say that *God* will do? (v. 15b)

    c. How might this verse (this promise) help you to follow Paul's exhortation to forget what lies behind and instead reach forward to what lies ahead?

Oswald Chambers teaches the concept that we are to keep on walking forward until God checks. But when He checks, we are to find out what is wrong and put it right.

4. By what standard are they to keep living, according to verse 16?

   a. Obviously, like Paul, we don't know everything and understand everything about the Christian life as yet, but how will following his direction in verse 16 and trusting the promise in verse 15b give us peace and rest as we reach forward to what lies ahead?

Review this week's memory verse.

Day 3
Daily Facts
Read Philippians 3:17-21

In our chapter this week, we have looked at Paul's confidence in the past (Day 1), his confidence in the present (Day 2), and today we will look at his confidence in the future.

1. What directive was Paul able to confidently give the Philippians in verse 17?

Notice the word "Brethren." Again, we see Paul's love for these people. If we thought of Paul as someone who put his confidence in his flesh, we might think him prideful in this verse.

a. Paul spoke a similar word to the Corinthians in 1 Corinthians 4:15-16. In verse 15b, he revealed his heart for them. How did he see himself? Does this help you understand his ability to ask them to imitate him?

b. Is there someone to whom you can look as your example and pattern of godliness? Is anyone able to look to you as their pattern of godly living?

2. Again, we see Paul's heart in these verses. In verse 18, Paul tells us what makes him weep. What is it?

Paul was so pure in heart. Although he denounced the ways of these enemies of Christ, he wept over their state.

a. Paul says of these men that they are enemies of the cross. See what he says about the cross in 1 Corinthians 1:18.

The cross speaks of suffering, loss, and death. These men were concerned with life here and now.

b. What four observations did Paul make concerning these enemies of the cross in verse 19?

1.
2.
3.
4.

3. In contrast to what we see of these enemies of the cross of Christ, what does Paul teach in Galatians 5:24?

a. What was Paul's own testimony to the power of the cross in his life? Galatians 6:14 (What a contrast!)

b. Do you think that God wants us to live a life of abstinence, maybe in a commune situation, living only with Christians? What do you think it means to be crucified to the world?

4. Why, according to Philippians 3:20a, should our minds *not* be set on earthly things?

Hebrews 11 is a wonderful chapter that gives us mini-biographies of our spiritual ancestors. (You may want to read it today!) Dotted through the chapter are verses that describe the hope of our fathers.

a. How is Abraham described in Hebrews 11:9-10?

b. How does Hebrews 11:16 describe the country Abraham and his descendants looked for? And what does this verse say regarding God?

c. Have you ever considered yourself an alien here in this land because you are looking for a heavenly home? How might this help you in your thinking?

5. What should be our hope as we remain here on this earth? Philippians 3:20b

    a. What, according to verse 21, will take place when our Savior returns for his children?

Oh what a glorious statement! How high are these words They are above and beyond us. They describe the one and only Sovereign Savior who is all-powerful.

Here we see the fulfillment of the hope that is in Paul's heart when he says, "In order that I may attain to the resurrection from the dead," speaking of that moment when Christ—by the power that He has even to subject all things to Himself—will transform each and every believer from his lowly earthly state into conformity with the body of His glory! Hallelujah and praise His name!

Review this week's memory verse.

Day 4
Overview of Philippians 3

Today we will be looking at the passage we have studied this week as a whole. The goal is to find the main lessons the Lord has for us from this chapter. Don't worry about being clever or profound—just do your best!

Find the Facts ...

1. See if you can state the *content* of this week's passage in a couple of sentences. (Who is speaking, what is taking place, what is the main subject?)

Look for the Heart ...

2. What do you think is the main *lesson* of this chapter? (What spiritual truths are taught here? Look for a command, a word of exhortation, a promise, etc.)

Hear Him Speak ...

3. Look for a *personal application* from the content of this chapter. It should come from the lesson you got from the chapter (question 2). How will you apply the lesson to yourself?

4. Was there a particular verse that ministered to you this week? What was it and how did it minister to you?

5. Write out your stone of remembrance *from memory*!

PHILIPPIANS 4

✤

Day 1
Daily Facts
Read Philippians 4:1-5

As Paul begins his final words to the Philippians, we again see his great love for them.

1.   Share the names Paul calls them in verse 1.

The word *crown* is the Greek word "stephanos" and speaks of the runner's wreath or victor's crown.

   a.   How does Paul express this same idea in his letter to the Thessalonians? Read 1 Thessalonians 2:19-20.

   b.   Read 1 Corinthians 3:12-14. Can you understand what Paul means when he speaks of them as his crown?

Verse 2 brings us right back to where we started in chapter 1. We must always remember as we study Philippians that it is actually a letter. Paul wrote this letter with a purpose—actually two main purposes—both which will be brought forth in this chapter.

It's a thank you letter, with a plea for unity, in particular in regard to an actual situation—the problem between Euodia and Syntyche.

2. What word of exhortation does Paul give Euodia and Syntyche in verse 2?

Paul's exhortation here is strong: NKJ—implore; NIV—plead; NAS—urge; Amp—entreat and advise.

    a. Considering Paul's words, as well as the intent of his whole letter, just how dangerous did he perceive this problem to be to the church?

Paul asks them to live in harmony (NASB). In the NKJ, this thought is translated to be *of the same mind*. This same thought was expressed in chapter 2.

3. Look again at Philippians 2:3-4 and share Paul's exhortation there.

    a. Who is our example in this? 2:5

Do you realize how much damage your selfishness and dissention in the body of Christ can cause? If you think you stand alone and that your attitudes and actions don't matter much, consider this entire letter and the place it has in the Bible for eternity. That is how important the subject of unity is to the body of Christ.

    b. See if you can come up with a word that you think best fulfills the root cause of Eudoia's and Syntyche's problem.

In verse 3, Paul asks another person to help in the cause of these women's reconciliation. It is not known for certain to whom Paul was speaking, but it might be Epaphroditus—who would deliver this letter and then be in a position to encourage the brethren. In this verse, we see the important position in ministry these women had. That is one reason the exhortation is so strong.

4. In verse 4, Paul brings us back to his theme of rejoicing. When exactly were they to rejoice according to this verse?

    a. Notice that their rejoicing was in the Lord. Does that give you any insight as to why we are able to rejoice always?

5. What is the next exhortation given in verse 5? (This command is in direct connection with Paul's word to Euodia and Syntyche.)

The Greek word for *forbearing spirit* (NASB) is difficult to translate. Some of the possibilities are "gentleness, unselfishness, considerateness, graciousness, yieldedness, and sweet reasonableness."

    a. Rather than being harshly dogmatic and unyielding, why is it always best in our dealings with others to have an attitude that is unselfish, gentle, and yielded?

    b. Could your attitude in relation to others be generally characterized as sweetly reasonable? Might there be some changes in perspective that you need to make? Why don't you decide to handle the next situation that arises with this kind of spirit?

Stone of Remembrance:

"I can do all things through Christ who strengthens me." Philippians 4:13

Day 2
Daily Facts
Read Philippians 4:6-9

1. Paul has already told us to rejoice always, now he exhorts us about being anxious. When is it all right to be anxious?

   a. Instead of being anxious—what are we to do?

   b. In what circumstances should this be our practice and perspective?

The song says, "Don't worry, be happy," Paul says, "Don't worry—pray!"

2. Why is there no actual help in telling someone "Don't worry, be happy"?

   a. Why is there great help in telling someone, "Don't worry, pray"?

The enemy will keep us focused on our problems rather than on God. Prayer gives us a correct focus.

3. Read Isaiah 42:5 to get a picture of the God to whom you are to make your requests.

a. What does Jeremiah 32:17 and 27 tell us about our God?

b. Challenge: For a new sense of the greatness of our God, read Job 38-42:6. Share something of what you gain from this.

4. What will happen when we take our minds off of our difficulties and deliberately ask God to intervene on our behalf? v. 7

a. What do you think is the basis on which this miracle will take place? See Hebrews 11:6.

b. If you pray and then begin to worry again, do you think you will remain at peace? What must you do?

c. What wonderful promise and help are we given in Proverbs 3:5-6?

Verse 8 gives us a wonderful aid in our pursuit of trusting God and leaning not on our own understanding. Again—remember that the enemy will attempt with all his strength to keep us focused on our difficulties (but remember also—greater is He who is in us!).

5. What things are we to dwell on according to verse 8? Whatever is:

The Amplified Bible says that we are to "think on, weigh and take account of these things [fix your minds on them]." That takes our work! No one will or can do this for us!

The words "whatever is true" speak of that which is actually true or real (genuine and exact), not what could possibly be true or real in some other situation or time of life.

   a. Are you prone to think about what might happen or what could happen rather than what is actually happening? In other words, do you worry about the possibilities of the future? How can this verse help you?

   b. Why do you think it would help you personally to dwell on what is true, honorable, right, pure, lovely, admirable, excellent, and worthy of praise?

   c. What does Proverbs 23:7a say on this subject?

6. In verse 9, the Philippians, once again, are given Paul as their earthly role model. What are they to practice?

There is an important principle here: Paul didn't just talk—he lived.

   a. What would be theirs as they followed his example of godly living?

Verses 6-7 tell us how to have the peace of God; verse 9 tells us how to have the God of peace!

Review this week's memory verse.

Day 3
Daily Facts
Read Philippians 4:10-23

Paul begins this section with a heart of thanksgiving, rejoicing in their concern for him that was revealed in their monetary gift. And yet, although he was thankful for their gift, he used this opportunity to share with them something he himself had learned.

1. Did Paul consider himself to be in need at the time when the gift arrived? How does he describe his perspective on this? v. 11

   a. Paul further describes his contentment in verse 12. In what circumstances could he live contentedly?

   b. What secret had he learned? v. 12b

In the Greek this word for *learned* (verse 12) is not the typical word used for this concept. It is "memyemai" and is used only here in the New Testament. It is actually an expression that was used in the pagan mystery religions and meant *to initiate* (speaking of initiating into the mysteries).

Paul's use of this particular word seems to point to his own initiation by experience into the secret of contentment.

> c. For a better understanding of the process of Paul's initiation into the secret of contentment, look at 2 Corinthians 1:8; 2:4; 4:8-10; 6:4-10; 7:5; 11:23-28; and 12:7. Share your insight into this.

2. Why is it that Paul could be content in any and every circumstance? Philippians 4:13

This is the key to the entire chapter! Was Paul content that he could take care of himself in any and every circumstance? No! He was content that Christ would give him what he needed to go through whatever came his way. The Amplified Bible puts it this way: "I am self-sufficient in Christ's sufficiency."

> a. Who do you look to for contentment: Yourself and your circumstances or Jesus Christ? How could Paul's personal perspective in verse 13 help you learn to be anxious for nothing and content in whatever circumstances you find yourself?

3. In verse 14, Paul again commends the Philippians for sending their gift and sharing in his affliction. The idea here is that they had fellowship with him in his suffering. How had they helped him before now? vv. 15-16

a. 2 Corinthians 8:1-4 gives us an important piece of information that we don't get in this letter. What does it reveal to us about the Philippians (one of the Macedonian churches) themselves?

b. How does Paul describe this sacrificial gift of the Philippians in 4:18b?

How seldom we give sacrificially. We should let the Philippians be an example to us in this. They didn't bless Paul out of their abundance but out of their deep poverty, and their gift rose to heaven as a well-pleasing sacrifice and a pleasant aroma.

Why don't you look for an opportunity to give sacrificially as an act of worship to God? (It doesn't have to be money—it could be sharing a talent or maybe the gift of your time.)

4. In receiving, as in everything, Paul has a higher perspective. Rather than concentrating on what their gift means to him, what is his perspective on the gift that they have given? v. 17

a. How does Paul describe his own position after receiving their sacrificial gift? v. 18a

It might be something worth considering that Paul was still locked in prison as he says, "I have everything I need" (Amplified), and (in the NASB), "an abundance."

b. How do these words, again, relate to Paul's outlook as expressed in verse 11?

c. Consider your own situation today. Could you say with Paul, "I have everything I need and am amply supplied" (Amp)? What if you couldn't buy one more thing (for your house, yard, family's wardrobe, etc.) for the next 6 months or a year? Could you be content?

5. What understanding enabled Paul to be content and see himself amply supplied at this moment, with no realization of what the future would hold? v. 19

a. Do you believe verses 13 and 19? What difference would it make in your life personally if you really believed these verses? Take a moment with this. Share with your own life and circumstance in mind.

What a high note to end on. Paul has exhorted us to so much through this wonderful letter—to unity, to humility, to heavenly mindedness, and now to contentment in Christ.

"Now to our God and Father be the glory forever and ever. Amen … The grace of the Lord Jesus Christ be with your Spirit." —Paul

Review this week's memory verse.

Day 4
Overview of Philippians 4

Today we will be looking at the passage we have studied this week as a whole. The goal is to find the main lessons the Lord has for us from this chapter. Don't worry about being clever or profound—just do your best!

Find the Facts ...

1. See if you can state the *content* of this week's passage in a couple of sentences. (Who is speaking, what is taking place, what is the main subject?)

Look for the Heart ...

2. What do you think is the main *lesson* of this chapter? (What spiritual truths are taught here? Look for a command, a word of exhortation, a promise, etc.)

Hear Him Speak ...

3. Look for a *personal application* from the content of this chapter. It should come from the lesson you got from the chapter (question 2). How will you apply the lesson to yourself?

4. Was there a particular verse that ministered to you this week? What was it and how did it minister to you?

5. Write out your stone of remembrance *from memory*!

ABOUT THE AUTHOR

✢

Linda has dedicated her life to serving the Lord as a teacher, writer, and speaker. While teaching the Word of God, training leaders, and speaking at retreats and other women's ministry functions, she has also written curriculum for over 20 books of the Bible.

If you would be interested in having more information about her ministry, please visit her blog at www.lindaoborne.wordpress.com, or email her at myutmost1@aol.com.

www.ingramcontent.com/pod-product-compliance
Lightning Source LLC
Chambersburg PA
CBHW060619030426

42337CB00018B/3118